START
Talking

The Seasons

First published in the UK in 2004 by
QED Publishing
A division of Quarto Publishing plc
The Fitzpatrick Building
188-194 York Way, London N7 9QP

A Catalogue record for this book is available from the British Library.

ISBN 1 84538 001 0

Written by Ian Smith
Designed by Zeta Jones
Editor Hannah Ray
Picture Researcher Joanne Beardwell

Creative Director Louise Morley
Editorial Manager Jean Coppendale
Series Consultant Anne Faundez

Printed and bound in China

Picture credits

Key: t = top, b = bottom, m = middle, c = centre, l = left, r = right

Corbis/Tom Bean 12–13, 22b, /Michael Boys 6–7, 22t, /Donna Disario 4–5, 23t,
/George McCarthy 20–21, /Tom Stewart 15; **Getty Images**/Phil Boorman 16–17,
/Daniel Bosier 11, /Jan Tove Johansson 14, /Richard Price 18, 23b, /Philip & Karen
Smith 10, /Alexander Walter 19.

The Seasons

Ian Smith

QED Publishing

Spring

Summer

The weather changes during the year. These changes are called seasons.

Autumn

Winter

Most countries have four seasons – spring, summer, autumn and winter.

Spring

In spring, the weather warms up and flowers begin to come out.

Yellow daffodils nod their heads at the sun.

Rain showers help the flowers to grow.

7

Spring

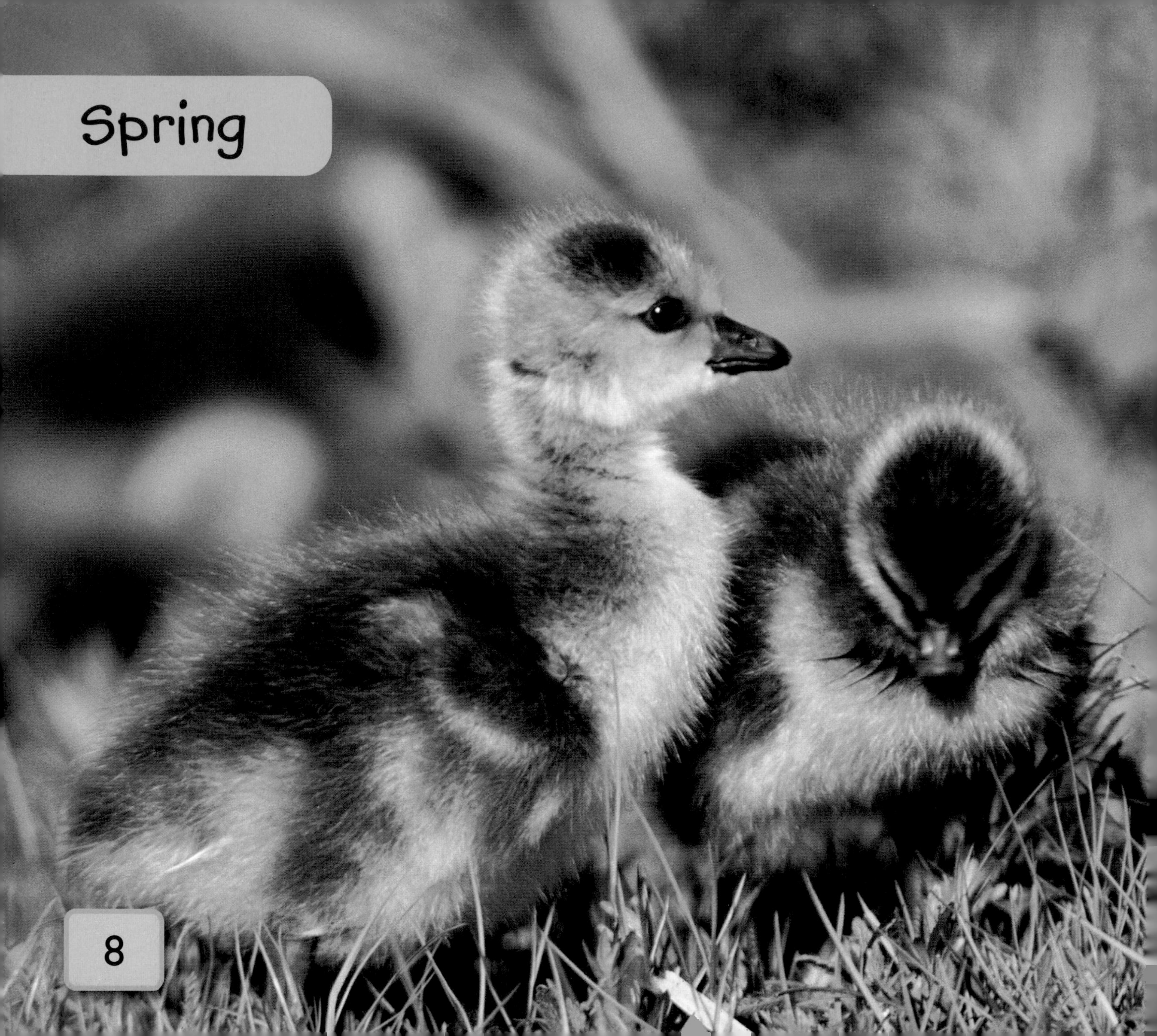

Lots of animals have their babies in spring.

Can you name the baby animals on this page?

Summer

After spring comes summer.
Phew! It is hot.

In summer, we can play outside and eat ice-creams.

Summer

In summer, fields are full of ripe, golden corn. Farmers can now harvest the corn to make bread.

13

Autumn

14

It is cooler in autumn.
Sometimes it is foggy
and we cannot see far.

The wind blows things
about during autumn.
Look at this kite!

15

Autumn

16

The leaves on lots of trees change colour. They turn from green to brown, orange and red. Then the leaves fall off the trees.

Do you like walking through the leaves like this?

Scrunch! Scrunch!

Winter

Brr! It is cold in winter. You need to wear lots of warm clothes.

Sometimes it snows. Hooray!
Do you like playing in the snow?

Winter

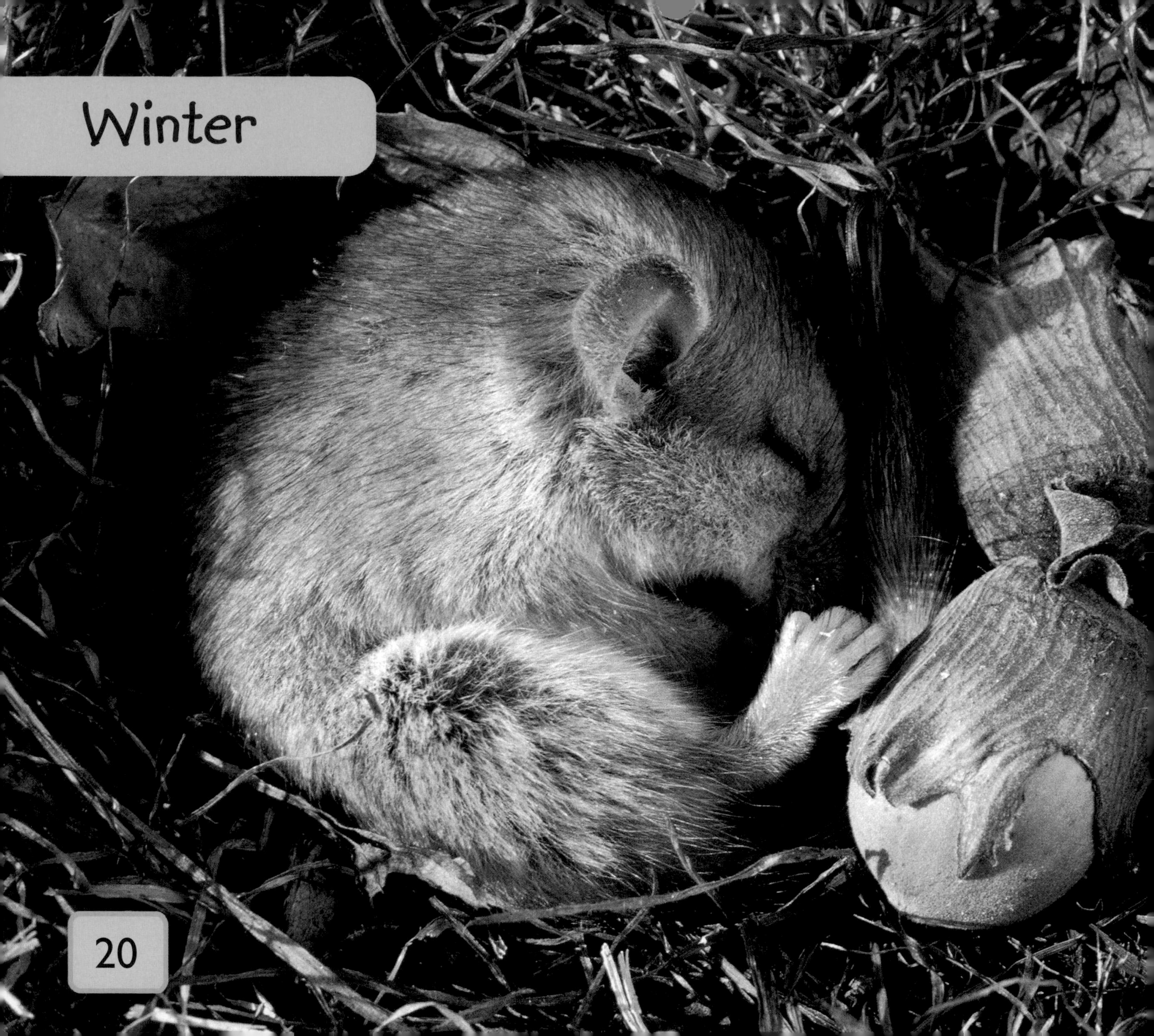

In winter, many birds fly
away to warmer countries.

Some animals have a long,
deep sleep. They do not
wake up until spring.

21

These flowers come out in the spring. What colour are they?

Can you remember what is happening in this picture?

In autumn, the leaves turn to which colours?

Why do you have to wear lots of warm clothes in winter?

23

Carers' and teachers' notes

- Use the pictures to prompt your child to talk about the activities and feelings that he/she associates with each season.
- As you read the book, you could both act out appropriate movements and facial expressions. For example, arm movements for trees blowing in the wind, or for tumbling leaves.
- Talk about the colours mentioned in the text, e.g. yellow daffodils, brown, orange and red leaves. Look at the photographs in the book. What colours can your child see? What colour is the snowman?
- Can your child recognize the baby animals on pages 8–9? What are they called? (They are ducklings.) What noises do they make? How do they move?
- Looking at the photographs on pages 4–5, point out the differences between the tree in summer and the tree in winter.
- Talk about the pictures showing summer scenes on pages 10–11. What is happening in the photographs?
- Ask your child to talk about other things that he/she enjoys about the summer. For example, having an ice-lolly, going barefoot, splashing in a paddling pool.
- Explain that ripe corn is used to make bread.
- Encourage your child to act out walking through dried leaves, saying 'Scrunch! Scrunch!' in time to the stamping of his/her feet.
- Make a collage to represent the current season – for example, arrange autumn leaves in a pattern.
- Talk about the clothes that your child might wear to keep warm. How does he/she keep warm indoors?
- Explain that the seasons are cyclical, and that spring follows on from winter. What time of year is it now? Will the dormouse on page 20 be awake or asleep?
- Test your child's understanding of the text by asking him/her to name an image from each season.
- Look at pages 22–23 and, together, discuss possible answers to the questions. Help your child to look back through the book to check your answers.